Cloud
Is a Piece of Cake

Cloud
Is a Piece of Cake

Febin John James

Notion Press

Old No. 38, New No. 6
McNichols Road, Chetpet
Chennai - 600 031

First Published by Notion Press 2016
Copyright © Febin John James 2016
All Rights Reserved.

ISBN 978-1-946204-92-9

Dedication

Anand Satyan

Naresh Annangar

Sharath Acharya

Nilufer Dmello

Sowmya Iyengar

Contents

Preface

The evolution of cloud technology has drastically reduced the time and effort to ship an idea to the market. You neither need costly physical servers nor expensive maintenance engineers. Moving to the cloud takes care of everything. The best part is you only pay for what you use. This is a boon for individual developers and start-ups.

The idea of writing this book occurred to me when I found out, that a lot of computer science students in India only knew about the cloud in theory. I had conducted interviews to hire engineers to my company and the companies in which I worked as a consultant. I could hardly find developers with cloud skills. The problem of unemployment in this country is not because of lack of jobs, but the lack of industry skills.

This book is what I lacked a few years ago when I started my career. You will learn how simple it is to build services on the cloud. It takes you from executing Unix commands to scaling your app.

Having cloud skills can attract job opportunities. Otherwise you always have the option to start up.

Let this book take you places ☺

"Febin does a brilliant job of introducing cloud computing jargon in layman's terms while at the same time carefully guiding the reader in getting started in building cloud apps practically without spoon feeding him/her."

Naresh Annangar, Sr. Security Researcher, Zscaler

"Cloud computing is no more the future; It is the present. From playing a game on Facebook to reading an e-book on a Kindle, everything is driven by cloud computing around us. This book makes learning fun, interesting and you get to solve real world problems .If you are a wannapreneur, entrepreneur, a student or someone who wants to start off with cloud computing, then this book is for you. Beware this book gets you addicted to cloud computing!"

Vishnu Sosale, Android Developer, HackerEarth

Thank You

For everything

Lord God Almighty

For your prayers

H.G. Dr. Abraham Mar Seraphim

For your love

Fr James Eapen, Mariamma James, Jenin Thomas James

For the book review

Prasanna Krishnamoorthy, Naresh Annangar

For the beautiful book cover

Prajiv T Varughese

For the support

Anand Satyan, Naresh Annangar, Sharath Acharya, Nilufer Dmello, Sowmya Iyengar, Vishwa Swaroop, Rajesh Mane, Arpith P Muddi

For the lessons in computer science

Ramesh Rao, Late Sumod V.K

For the mentorship

Ravi G Narayan, Prathibha Sastry, Prasanna Krishnamoorthy, Microsoft Ventures

For the inspiration

Elisabeth Robson, George Alexander, St. Aloysius College

For the appreciation

Dr Thomas P John, Dr Shikha Tiwari, T John College, St Mary's Orthodox Church Begur, Thomas Tharakan, Asha Biju, St Gregorios Cathedral Youth, Namma Bengaluru Foundation

For the fun times

Emma Ann George, Abhiya, Daryl, Jacob P Abraham, Angel Mary Thomas, Janet K Verghese, Jenson K Verghese, Ansu Ann Thomas, Alexander Philip, Verghese P Abraham, Abhilash Jose, Abraham, Meera Abraham, Anith John, Fr. PC Philip, Annie Philip, Giju Mathew, Ashin Paul, Abraham Mathews, Anil Amesur, Harish Balan, Dharam Chheda, Sara Mary Philip, Deepak, Gent Philip Mathew, Prajiv T Varughese, Hridya Varughese, Merin Mercy Mathew, Abin Iype, Naveen Peter, Viji Mary Jobi, Jeff George, Sharon Saji, Jibin Varghese, Errol B Tauro, Eeeshan Achar, Ananth Kamath, Nikhil Bhandary, Pranav Narayan, Prashanth, Murugavel Vel, Jitender Choudhary,Poornesh Kumar, Aby Varghese, Chris Rohit Brendan, Sathish V J, Varsha, Swetha Jacob, Fr. Joe, Reeja Joe, Denil Thomas, Johny K Joseph, Fr Bejoy, Libin Varghese, Liju Raj, Reuben Jacob, Shebin, Jessica, Sheena, Geo Joy, Geo Mathew, Mohammed Rafeeq, Swagath, Prajwal, Vinay, Ravi, Pavan, Hemanth, Anil Koshy, Jom Thomas, Steffi Thambi, Neha Anna Johny, Robin Babu, Rijo Geevarghese, Fr.Philip Kuruvila, Bibi Kuruvila, Jocelyn, Liju Varghese, Rini Varghese,

Vishnu Shoshale, Santhu, Lakshmi Ananth, Anand H, Shagufta Mehmood, Deepak Panigrahy, Ram Papineni, Sandip Kumar, Niketh Sabbineni, Ajay Narang, Aditya Bandi, Sarang Lakare, Kunal, Nikhil, Aadhesh,Sandeep, Ramkumar Nandakumar, Gautam Tambay, Keertana Ravi, Pavan, Sheetal, Mahesh Subramanian, Laxman Papineni, Nemesh Singh, Khushal Patel, Ram Sahasranam,Parul Gupta, Souvik Dutta, Ashwin Nagarajan.

What Will the Book Teach You?

What is in this book?

Ever wondered how apps like Uber, Whatsapp, Snapchat, Instagram, Feedly, etc. work? Uber provides you locations of available cars real-time. Whatsapp and Snapchat let you send texts, photos and videos instantly. Instagram enables you to share photos. Feedly gives you news of your interest. This book teaches you to build such cloud apps.

Who is the book for?

1. You are a computer science student looking to learn industry skills.
2. You have basic coding skills and want to learn cloud development.
3. You are a software engineer with years of experience but don't understand the cloud.

4. You want to move your service to cloud.
5. You want to develop cloud apps.

What all things do I require?

You will need basic programming skills in Python, JavaScript and understand simple SQL queries. If you can write a program using functions, classes and make an SQL query with a 'where' condition, you are good to go. If not I would suggest you take free courses on Code Academy. You will also need an AWS (Amazon Web Services) account. You can use a debit card to activate the account. You don't have to pay anything since we are sticking to free tier. Though we are making use of AWS in this book, once you understand the underlying concepts you will be able to replicate them in any cloud providers such as Microsoft Azure, Rackspace, Digital Ocean, etc.

What if I don't have an AWS account?

Then all you need is an Ubuntu operating system.

What will I learn?

Introduction to Cloud

So you want to host your service on the internet. We will see how web services work, the problems with hosting physicals servers and why the cloud is efficient. We'll also discuss different types of cloud services such as Infrastructure as a service, Platform as a service and Software as a service.

Set up a virtual machine

This chapter teaches you to make a virtual machine sing and dance. We will see how we can connect to our remote computer, execute Unix commands, copy files, run scheduled jobs, do bash scripting, etc. By the end of this chapter, you will deploy a web page on an Apache server.

Build a News Reader App – Part 1

We will build a news reader app which aggregates news from different sources and serves them to users. We will learn how to architect a cloud service, save time using existing resources and finally make an API for our news reader app.

Build a News Reader App – Part 2

Here we will create a user interface for our news reader app. We will learn to make asynchronous requests and update the view without refreshing the web page. By the end of the chapter, you will deploy the news reader app. You will be able to share the app with your friends.

Scale It up

Our news reader app has gone viral. We will see to handle such situations by learning about load balancing, horizontal and vertical scaling.

Secure your cloud app

In this chapter, we will see how to counter attacks. We will learn about Security Aware Coding, Encryption, SQL Injections and Requests Limiting.

This book is different

Short and Sweet

This book won't bore you with bulk information. It explains only about what is required in a simple language. You will learn the rest by doing it physically.

Challenges

The book has got 'Do It Yourself' challenges. These challenges are designed to increase your skill. The methods of implementing things on cloud change day by day. However, once you understand the underlying concepts, you can apply it easily. This book enforces that.

What if I get stuck?

Try googling your problem. Most of the time Stack Over Flow will have the answer to your problem. I have also created a Google group to help you. You can post your question there; I will personally answer them.

```
https://groups.google.com/forum/#!forum/cloud-is-a-
piece-of-cake/
```

Earn Badges

After you complete each chapter, visit pieceofcakelabs.com/ cloud to finish challenges and earn badges.

The Comic Contest

Complete the comic exercise at the end of each chapter. Take photos of your comic strips and share them with the hashtag #CloudIsaPieceofCake. The best one will be featured in my next book.

Code

All the code used in this book is available in the following git repository.

```
https://github.com/jamesfebin/cloud_cake
```

About The Author

Febin John James is the Chief Technology Officer of Boutline (Infootball). He also works as a tech consultant. He has conducted workshops on cloud computing since his college days. He had the opportunity to work with several tech start-ups during his tenure at the Microsoft Ventures Acceleration Program. He has also bagged devices, cash prizes and recognition from companies like Intel, Blackberry and Microsoft.

Introduction to Cloud

Consider you wanted to host a movie booking service. Before cloud, you had to buy a physical server and host it. So whenever a customer wants to book a ticket, he sends a request from his computer to your server. The server processes the request and sends data back to the client (customer's computer). If the server and the client were having a conversation, it would look like this.

Client : *I need tickets for Captain America: Civil War.*

Server : *Here are the available seats for the movie {P1, P2, P4, A3 ...}*

Client : *I am booking P1, P2*

Server : *Blocking the seats, awaiting payment*

Client : *Here are my payment details {CardNo: XXXXXX, CVV...}*

Server : *Congrats, they are booked.*

The customer's computer and the server communicate with packets of data.

Your server would be able to handle 1000's of such requests based on its configuration.

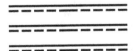

However, what happens when the demands exceed the server's limit? Say 10k - 20k requests? It is the same case when ten to twenty people are pinging you on Whatsapp. You will attempt to answer them all one by one. However, you would take a lot of time. However, on the internet this delay is unacceptable.

Why can't we add more servers?

Yes, that's a solution. Say you buy or rent ten more servers. Now they can work as a team and share the load. That works well. However, your service won't have such requests all the time. Compare the first day of the Civil War Movie to the fiftieth day. The number of requests drops down. The additional servers you bought are now jobless. You will be still paying for their electricity and bandwidth. In some situations, you can never predict when requests are at peak. So it's necessary for the servers to be ready. When the next peak time arrives, your servers may be outdated. Hosting it physically has a lot of other problems like power outages, maintenance cost, etc. Since this involves wastage of resources, this isn't an effective solution. The cloud was developed to tackle this.

How can the cloud help?

In the cloud, we have a shared pool of computer resources (servers, storage, applications, etc.) at our disposal. When you need more resources, all you need is to ask. Provisioning resources immediately is a piece of cake for the cloud. You can free resources when they are not needed. In this way, you only pay for what you use. Your cloud provider will take care of all the maintenance.

Where is the cloud?

The shared pool of computer resources exists in a physical location called data centers. Your cloud providers have multiple data centers around the world. So your data is replicated at multiple sites. Even if a data center goes down because of a natural calamity, it's still safe in another location.

What are IaaS, PaaS and SaaS?

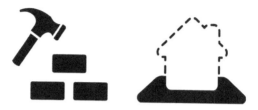

In IaaS (Infrastructure as a Service) you are given materials like cement, bricks, sheets, etc. to build a house. Similarly, here you get to choose the hardware you want to make the cloud service. You have got the flexibility to make it in the way you want. Ex: Amazon Web Services, Microsoft Azure, Google Compute Engine, etc.

In PaaS (Platform as a Service) the house is built for you, you only need to furnish it. Similarly, here you are provided preconfigured hardware. So it can only run applications it supports. You don't get the flexibility when compared with IAAS. Ex: Heroku, Google App Engine, etc.

In SaaS (Software as a Service) all you need to occupy. Here you are offered software on a subscription basis. Ex: Gmail, Yahoo, etc.

What do I need to get started?

You will need an activated Amazon Web Service Account. You don't have to pay anything since we will be sticking to free tier. If you are using Windows OS, please download Cygwin. That's all; you are good to go.

Set up a Virtual Machine

What is a virtual machine?

Imagine a huge room. It can be sub divided into smaller compartments. Similarly, a computer of large capacity can be subdivided into smaller compartments or virtual machines.

Each of these virtual machines feels like they have their own hardware. But, in reality, it doesn't. It imitates dedicated hardware. Since it's virtual, allocation and deallocation of resources are easy.

Note: In the top right of your AWS dashboard select the region which is closest to your location.

Create a Virtual Machine

AWS Dashboard

EC2 > Launch Instance

AWS ⌄ | Services ⌄ | Edit ⌄   Febin John James ⌄   N. California ⌄   Support ⌄

1. Choose AMI | 2. Choose Instance Type | 3. Configure Instance | 4. Add Storage | 5. Tag Instance | 6. Configure Security Group | 7. Review

Step 1: Choose an Amazon Machine Image (AMI)

Cancel and Exit

AWS Marketplace

Community AMIs

☑ Free tier only ⓘ

Amazon Linux
Free tier eligible

The Amazon Linux AMI is an EBS-backed, AWS-supported image. The default image includes AWS command line tools, Python, Ruby, Perl, and Java. The repositories include Docker, PHP, MySQL, PostgreSQL, and other packages.

Root device type: ebs   Virtualization type: hvm

64-bit

Red Hat Enterprise Linux 7.2 (HVM), SSD Volume Type - ami-d1315fb1

Red Hat
Free tier eligible

Red Hat Enterprise Linux version 7.2 (HVM), EBS General Purpose (SSD) Volume Type

Root device type: ebs   Virtualization type: hvm

Select
64-bit

SUSE Linux Enterprise Server 12 SP 1 (HVM), SSD Volume Type - ami-6d701b0d

SUSE Linux
Free tier eligible

SUSE Linux Enterprise Server 12 Service Pack 1 (HVM), EBS General Purpose (SSD) Volume Type. Public Cloud, Advanced Systems Management, Web and Scripting, and Legacy modules enabled.

Root device type: ebs   Virtualization type: hvm

Select
64-bit

Ubuntu Server 14.04 LTS (HVM), SSD Volume Type - ami-06116566

Ubuntu
Free tier eligible

Ubuntu Server 14.04 LTS (HVM), EBS General Purpose (SSD) Volume Type. Support available from Canonical (http://www.ubuntu.com/cloud/services).

Root device type: ebs   Virtualization type: hvm

Select
64-bit

Select Instance OS

Here we select the OS of our virtual machine. We will be using Ubuntu. Select Ubuntu Server (Make sure it's free-tier eligible as shown in the image).

Step 2: Choose an Instance Type

Amazon EC2 provides a wide selection of instance types optimized to fit different use cases. Instances are virtual servers that can run applications. They have varying combinations of CPU, memory, storage, and networking capacity, and give you the flexibility to choose the appropriate mix of resources for your applications. Learn more about instance types and how they can meet your computing needs.

Filter by: All instance types ⌄ Current generation ⌄ Show/Hide Columns

Currently selected: t2.micro (Variable ECUs, 1 vCPUs, 2.5 GHz, Intel Xeon Family, 1 GiB memory, EBS only)

	Family	Type	vCPUs (i)	Memory (GiB)	Instance Storage (GB) (i)	EBS-Optimized Available (i)	Network Performance (i)
	General purpose	t2.nano	1	0.5	EBS only	-	Low to Moderate
●	General purpose	t2.micro Free tier eligible	1	1	EBS only	-	Low to Moderate
	General purpose	t2.small	1	2	EBS only	-	Low to Moderate
	General purpose	t2.medium	2	4	EBS only	-	Low to Moderate
	General purpose	t2.large	2	8	EBS only	-	Low to Moderate

Cancel Previous **Review and Launch** **Next: Configure Instance Details**

Select Instance Type

Here we choose the configuration of our virtual machine. Select t2.micro or whichever is free-tier. Click Review and Launch.

1. Choose AMI   2. Choose Instance Type   3. Configure Instance   4. Add Storage   5. Tag Instance   6. Configure Security Group   **7. Review**

Step 7: Review Instance Launch

▼ AMI Details   Edit AMI

🅒 **Ubuntu Server 14.04 LTS (HVM), SSD Volume Type - ami-06116566**

| Free for eligible | Ubuntu Server 14.04 LTS (HVM), EBS General Purpose (SSD) Volume Type. Support available from Canonical (http://www.ubuntu.com/cloud/services). |

Root Device Type: ebs   Virtualization type: hvm

▼ Instance Type   Edit instance type

Instance Type	ECUs	vCPUs	Memory (GiB)	Instance Storage (GB)	EBS-Optimized Available	Network Performance
t2.micro	Variable	1	1	EBS only	-	Low to Moderate

▼ Security Groups   Edit security groups

Security group name   launch-wizard-1
Description   launch-wizard-1 created 2016-06-23T21:11:49.568+05:30

Type ⓘ	Protocol ⓘ	Port Range ⓘ	Source ⓘ
SSH	TCP	22	0.0.0.0/0

Cancel   Previous   **Launch**

Review and Launch

Here you can see security groups. Security groups allow you to restrict VM usage to specific IP. For now, it's fine. Leave it that way. Click on launch to start the instance.

Select an existing key pair or create a new key pair ✕

A key pair consists of a **public key** that AWS stores, and a **private key file** that you store. Together, they allow you to connect to your instance securely. For Windows AMIs, the private key file is required to obtain the password used to log into your instance. For Linux AMIs, the private key file allows you to securely SSH into your instance.

Note: The selected key pair will be added to the set of keys authorized for this instance. Learn more about removing existing key pairs from a public AMI.

Create a new key pair

Key pair name

myec2instance

Download Key Pair

⚹ You have to download the **private key file** (*.pem file) before you can continue. **Store it in a secure and accessible location.** You will not be able to download the file again after it's created.

Cancel   **Launch Instances**

Create a new key pair

Key pair allows you to connect to your instance securely instead of a password. Download the key pair file and keep it safe. Once you have downloaded the key pair, you can click Launch Instances.

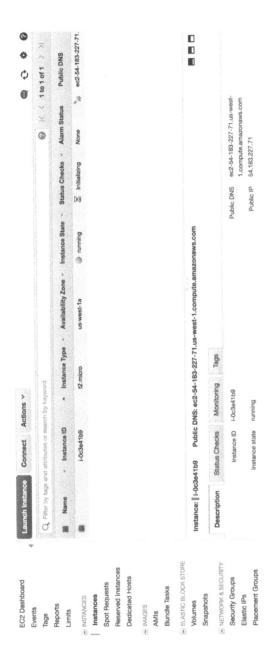

Instances

Now, wait till instance state is 'running'. Then you are ready to go. Now we will use the public IP shown in the image to connect to our EC2 instance.

Connect to an EC2 Instance (Virtual Machine)

If you are using a Linux or a Mac OS

You will need to navigate to the folder containing the downloaded key pair on your terminal. I assume it's in your Downloads folder. If you are not sure how to do this, please paste the file to your Downloads folder. Later in this chapter, you will master the bash commands.

```
cd ~/Downloads
chmod 400 myec2instance.pem
ssh -i myec2instance.pem ubuntu@54.183.227.71
```

If you are using a Windows OS

Download and install Cygwin. Paste the key file inside C:\ cygwin\home\username; this might be different in case you have changed your root directory. Once you paste it in the root directory, run the following commands.

```
chmod 400 myec2instance.pem
ssh -i myec2instance.pem ubuntu@54.183.227.71
```

Connect to an EC2 Instance

```
Downloads — ubuntu@ip-172-31-9-17: ~ — ssh — 132×31

Macbook:downloads user$ ssh -i myec2instance.pem ubuntu@54.183.227.71
The authenticity of host '54.183.227.71 (54.183.227.71)' can't be established.
RSA key fingerprint is fd91:ad:10:54:c8:9c:a3:c4:b1:9c:e9i36:d5:88:3b.
Are you sure you want to continue connecting (yes/no)? yes
Warning: Permanently added '54.183.227.71' (RSA) to the list of known hosts.
Welcome to Ubuntu 14.04.3 LTS (GNU/Linux 3.13.0-74-generic x86_64)

 * Documentation:  https://help.ubuntu.com/

  System information as of Wed Jul 13 06:49:47 UTC 2016

  System load:  0.0               Processes:           101
  Usage of /:   11.6% of 7.74GB   Users logged in:     0
  Memory usage: 0%                IP address for eth0: 172.31.9.17
  Swap usage:   0%

  Graph this data and manage this system at:
    https://landscape.canonical.com/

  Get cloud support with Ubuntu Advantage Cloud Guest:
    http://www.ubuntu.com/business/services/cloud

91 packages can be updated.
54 updates are security updates.


Last login: Wed Jul 13 06:49:49 2016 from 122.172.55.16
ubuntu@ip-172-31-9-17:~$
```

Unix Commands

What is Unix?

Unix is an operating system, which was developed at AT&T Bell Laboratories in the 1960s. It has constantly been evolving since then. It's a robust, multi-user, multi-tasking system for servers, laptops, and PCs.

What is Linux?

Linux is a Unix-like Operating System. It behaves like a Unix System. Linux has got many distributions like Fedora, OpenSUSE, Ubuntu, etc. Our VM runs on Ubuntu operating system.

What are Unix commands?

 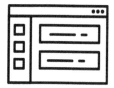

Operating systems have got two types of interfaces - Character User Interface (CUI) and Graphical User Interface (GUI). GUI is an interface most of the personal computers and laptops have with graphical icons and visual indicators. CUI is a text-based interface. MS-DOS on Windows and Terminal on MAC are examples of CUI. In CUI we can do more things in less time, and it consumes very less memory as well. However, in a text-based interface, we will need to learn the commands to interact with the operating system. Unix commands are used to communicate with a Unix-like operating system.

Before we continue

You can go forward in two ways. Either by going through the Unix commands section, learn by executing them or skipping to the Apache server section and coming back to this chapter when you need help with a Unix command.

Environment Variables

The operating system has got a lot of variables like current user, OS language, home directory location, etc. These are called environment variables. It's also possible for us to set environment variables. Hence the programs can handle situations differently for a particular environment condition.

Env

List all environment variablesEnv

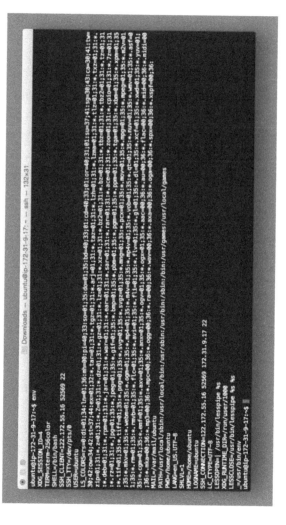

List of environment variables

Read an Environment Variable

```
echo $PATH
```

*/usr/local/sbin:/usr/local/bin:/usr/sbin:/usr/bin:/
sbin:/bin:/usr/\ games:/usr/local/games*

Write an Environment Variable

```
export WEATHER="Sunny"
```

```
echo $WEATHER
```

Sunny

Unix File System

Create a file

We will create a file inside myapp directory.

```
cd $HOME
touch home.html
```

Write to a file

Let's write a file. The following command opens nano editor, write "hello" inside it. Then press CTRL-O, enter to save the file and CTRL-X to exit the editor.

```
nano home.html
```

Read contents of a file

```
cat home.html
```

hello

Rename a file

Let's rename "home.html" to "index.html"

```
mv home.html index.html
```

Copy a file

Let's copy index.html to a new file called home.html

```
cp index.html home.html
```

List Files

This command will list all the files and directories in the current directory.

```
ls
```
home.html index.html

Rename a file

Let us rename "home.html" to "index.html"

```
mv home.html index.html
```

Remove a file

```
rm index.html
```

Directory

The directory in Unix System is like folders you have on your computer.

Print Working Directory

```
pwd
```
/home/ubuntu

Create Directory

Here we create two directories myapp and static_files.

```
mkdir myapp
mkdir static_files
```

Move Directory

Let us move staticfiles inside the myapp folder.

```
mv static_files myapp
```

Change Directory

We will go inside the myapp directory.

```
cd myapp
```

List

This command will list all the files and directories in the current directory.

```
ls
static_files
```

Remove Directory

Removes a directory

```
rmdir static_files
```

File Permissions

Users

Linux is a multi-user operating system. Mainly Linux users are of three types: super users, system users and normal users. Normal users are human users who log in to the run system programs interactively. System users are created to run specific applications such as background processes which don't need interaction. Each user can access only files he is permitted to. The owner of the file grants permissions. However, there is another type of user called superuser or root user who can override any permission restrictions. In other words, he has access to anything on the server. We can also provide normal user accounts with superuser privileges.

List all users

List all the users in a server

```
cat /etc/passwd
```

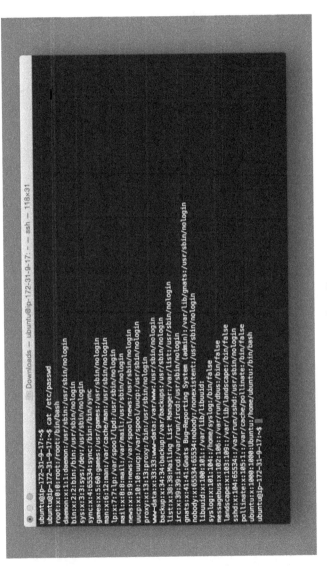

List all users

Groups

Groups are a collection of multiple users. By default user belongs to a group. He can also be a part of multiple groups.

List all groups

List all the groups in a server

```
cat /etc/group
```

List all groups

Permissions

There are three types of permissions. Read, Write and Execute. Read permissions are required when you need to view a file, write to modify and execute for running the file as a script or application.

List all permissions

List files with their permissions

```
cd /var/log
ls -l
```

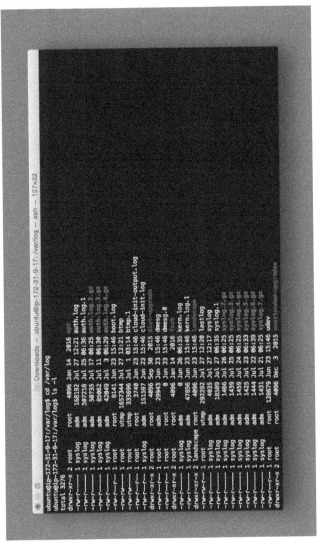

List files with their permissions

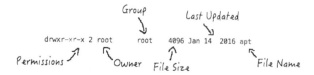

Permissions

Read	Write	Execute	No Permission
r	w	x	-

Let us take a closer look at permissions

Type	User	Group	Others
d	rwx	r-x	r-x

Here 'd' denotes it's a directory. If it's a file, it's denoted as '-'. As you see, the permissions are split into three parts. Permission for the user (owner of the file), members of file's group and others (Others here are any user who is not the owner of the file and is not a member of the group file belongs to). Here the user or the owner of the file has got permission 'rwx' which means he can read, write and execute. Group and Others have got permission 'r-x' which is read and executed. You won't be able to modify the file.

Changing File Permissions

Let's see how we can change file permissions. We will navigate to log files in the upstart folder

```
cd /var/log/upstart
ls -l
```

```
                        Downloads — ubuntu@ip-172-31-9-17: /var/log/upstart — ssh — 127×32
ubuntu@ip-172-31-9-17:~$ cd /var/log/upstart
ubuntu@ip-172-31-9-17:/var/log/upstart$ ls -l
total 48
-rw-r--r-- 1 root root  63 Jun 23 15:46 console-setup.log.1.gz
-rw-r--r-- 1 root root  66 Jun 23 15:46 container-detect.log.1.gz
-rw-r--r-- 1 root root  33 Jun 23 15:46 cryptdisks.log.1.gz
-rw-r--r-- 1 root root 344 Jun 23 15:46 network-interface-eth0.log.1.gz
-rw-r--r-- 2 root root 184 Jun 23 15:46 pollinate.log.1.gz
-rw-r--r-- 1 root root 204 Jun 23 15:46 procps-static-network-up.log.1.gz
-rw-r--r-- 1 root root 204 Jun 23 15:46 procps-virtual-filesystems.log.1.gz
-rw-r--r-- 1 root root  84 Jun 23 15:46 rsyslog.log.1.gz
-rw-r--r-- 1 root root 268 Jul 27 12:28 systemd-logind.log
-rw-r--r-- 1 root root  72 Jul 15 03:15 systemd-logind.log.1.gz
-rw-r--r-- 1 root root  86 Jul 13 13:17 systemd-logind.log.2.gz
-rw-r--r-- 1 root root 169 Jun 24 10:36 systemd-logind.log.3.gz
ubuntu@ip-172-31-9-17:/var/log/upstart$
```

Here systemd-logind.log file has got permission '-rw-r——'
which means only the root user can access the file. Let's try
accessing the file.

```
cat systemd-logind.log
cat: systemd-logind.log: Permission denied
```

We get a permission denied error. Ok, now let's change the
permission. We can do this only because our account has got
super user privileges (All accounts don't have this privilege
unless it's granted to them).

```
sudo chmod o+r systemd-logind.log
```

Here prefixing 'sudo' we are using our super user power.
Command 'chmod' is used to change the file permission.
Here in 'o+r', 'o' denotes other users (Who is neither the
owner of the file or belong to the group the file belongs to),
'+' denotes add permission, 'r' is read permission. So the
above command gives other users read permissions to the
file. Now let's try reading the file.

```
cat systemd-logind.log
```

```
● ● ●                    ⬚ Downloads — ubuntu@ip-172-31-9-17: /var/log/upstart — ssh — 127×32

ubuntu@ip-172-31-9-17:/var/log/upstart$ ls -l
total 48
-rw-r--r-- 1 root root  63 Jun 23 15:46 console-setup.log.1.gz
-rw-r--r-- 1 root root  66 Jun 23 15:46 containe-detect.log.1.gz
-rw-r--r-- 1 root root  33 Jun 23 15:46 cryptdisks.log.1.gz
-rw-r--r-- 1 root root 344 Jun 23 15:46 network-interface-eth0.log.1.gz
-rw-r--r-- 1 root root 184 Jun 23 15:46 pollinate.log.1.gz
-rw-r--r-- 1 root root 204 Jun 23 15:46 procps-static-network-up.log.1.gz
-rw-r--r-- 1 root root 204 Jun 23 15:46 procps-virtual-filesystems.log.1.gz
-rw-r--r-- 1 root root  84 Jun 23 15:46 rsyslog.log.1.gz
-rw-r--r-- 1 root root 260 Jul 27 12:20 systemd-logind.log
-rw-r--r-- 1 root root  72 Jul 15 03:15 systemd-logind.log.1.gz
-rw-r--r-- 1 root root  86 Jul 13 13:17 systemd-logind.log.2.gz
-rw-r--r-- 1 root root 169 Jun 24 10:36 systemd-logind.log.3.gz
ubuntu@ip-172-31-9-17:/var/log/upstart$ cat  systemd-logind.log
cat: systemd-logind.log: Permission denied
ubuntu@ip-172-31-9-17:/var/log/upstart$ sudo chmod o+r systemd-logind.log
ubuntu@ip-172-31-9-17:/var/log/upstart$ cat systemd-logind.log
Removed session 7.
New session 8 of user ubuntu.
New session 9 of user ubuntu.
Removed session 8.
Removed session 9.
New session 10 of user ubuntu.
Removed session 10.
New session 11 of user ubuntu.
Removed session 11.
New session 12 of user ubuntu.
ubuntu@ip-172-31-9-17:/var/log/upstart$ ▮
```

Now in order to remove the read permission we gave to other users.

```
sudo chmod o-r systemd-logind.log
```

In case you need to change the permission of the owner, say to remove write permissions then it will be 'u-w'. Where 'u' denotes the owner. You can do the same to a group using 'g-w' where 'g' denotes group.

File Search

First, we will navigate to a directory with a lot of files.

```
cd /var/log
```

Finding files

Let's search for the file "rsyslog.log.1.gz"

```
find . -name rsyslog.log.1.gz
```
```
./upstart/rsyslog.log.1.gz
```

Here '.' denotes search for files inside the current directory. Here we will need to specify the full name of the file.

Finding files with partial name match

```
find . -name "*.gz"
```
```
./syslog.6.gz ./syslog.3.gz ./syslog.5.gz
```

Here '*' is a wildcard character, '.gz' will give you the name of the files ending with '.gz'.

Search inside a file

Let us look up for the word 'client' inside 'syslog.1'.

```
grep client syslog.1
```

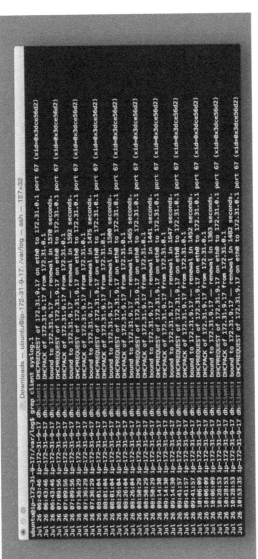

Search inside a file

Search inside folders and files

Let us look up for the word 'user' inside all folders and files in current directory.

`grep -nr user .`

Search inside folders and files

Here 'n' asks for line numbers, 'r' to search recursively inside all files and folders, '.' is to denote to search inside current directory.

This command will list all the files along with the lines containing 'user' in it.

SCP Command

Secure copy command allows you to copy files between servers. So let's try copying a file from our computer to the server. In order to do this, exit the session from the server by typing 'exit'. Go to the Downloads folder on your computer. We will create a file named 'examplefile.txt'. Then send it across to our ec2 instance.

```
touch examplefile.txt
scp -i myec2instance.pem examplefile.txt
ubuntu@54.183.227.71:/home/ubuntu
```

Now let's login to our ec2 instance. There you find the "examplefile.txt"

```
ssh -i myec2instance.pem ubuntu@54.183.227.71
ls
examplefile.txt myapp
```

Now let us create a file named "examplefile2.txt" and see how we can copy it to our computer.

```
touch examplefile2.txt
exit
scp   -i   myec2instance.pem   ubuntu@54.183.227.71:/home/
ubuntu/examplefile2.txt
```

Bash Scripting

We have learned a lot of commands. Let's write a bash script and run it. We will create a simple script which echoes 'hello world'. Make sure you are logged back into the server.

```
ssh -i myec2instance.pem ubuntu@54.183.227.71
nano hello.sh
```

Inside hello.sh

```
#!/bin/bash
echo Hello World
```

The first line tells the system it's a bash script. To save and exit the editor press CTRL-O, enter then CTRL-X.

Execute the bash script

```
bash hello.sh
Hello World
```

Script to Make Backup of a File Every Minute

Let us make a script while makes backup of a file every minute

```
cd $HOME
touch file.txt
touch backup.txt
nano copy.sh
```

Now let us write the bash script inside copy.sh

```
#!/bin/bash
cp /home/ubuntu/file.txt /home/ubuntu/backup.txt
```

To save the file and exit the editor CTRL-O, enter and CTRL-X

Now we need to make sure the script executed every minute. We can use crontab for that.

What is crontab?

Crontab is a time-based job scheduler. Hence can help us run scripts automatically as and when required. Every n minutes or hours or days or months etc.

```
sudo crontab -e
```

Choose nano editor or option 2, and then paste the following line in the bottom of the file, which tells the system to run the copy script every minute.

```
* * * * * bash /home/ubuntu/copy.sh
```

Now let us restart the cron service

```
sudo service cron restart
```

Now make changes to file.txt, wait for say two minutes. You will see the changes reflected in backup.txt

Installing Software Packages

What are Linux packages?

Linux packages are file archives containing all of the files needed for a particular application. All the Linux software comes in these packages.

For now, we need two packages git and apache2

```
sudo apt-get install git -y
sudo apt install apache2 -y
```

Apache Server

What is the apache server?

Apache is an open source web server that is used by most of the web servers around the world. A web server is similar to a receptionist who welcomes you and helps you with your requirement. Here a web server checks what the user has requested and serves him with web pages.

Currently, our EC2 instance disables any incoming traffic to our server. Our Apache server runs on port 80. We will need to add a security rule to allow connections on port 80.

Login to AWS portal > EC2 Instance > Security Groups

EC2 Dashboard
Events
Tags
Reports
Limits

☐ INSTANCES
Instances
Spot Requests
Reserved Instances
Dedicated Hosts

☐ IMAGES
AMIs
Bundle Tasks

☐ ELASTIC BLOCK STORE
Volumes
Snapshots

☐ NETWORK & SECURITY
Security Groups
Elastic IPs
Placement Groups
Key Pairs
Network Interfaces

☐ LOAD BALANCING
Load Balancers

Create Security Group   Actions ∨

Q Filter by tags and attributes or search by keyword   ❷ |< < 1 to 2 of 2 > >|

	Name	▾	Group ID	▲	Group Name	▾	VPC ID	▾	Description	▾
■			sg-7ded6719		launch-wizard-1		vpc-f47a1b91		launch-wizard-1 created 2016-06-23T21:1...	
☐			sg-93b2a1f6		default		vpc-f47a1b91		default VPC security group	

Description   **Inbound**   Outbound   Tags

Edit

Type ⓘ	Protocol ⓘ	Port Range ⓘ	Source ⓘ
SSH	TCP	22	0.0.0.0/0

Security Groups

Make sure launch wizard is selected then click on edit in the bottom.

Security Groups

Click on Add Rule. Select HTTP from the list > Save.

Edit Security Groups

Now go to your web browser. Navigate to http://Your Ec2InstanceIP

Apache2 Ubuntu Default Page

ubuntu

It works!

This is the default welcome page used to test the correct operation of the Apache2 server after installation on Ubuntu systems. It is based on the equivalent page on Debian, from which the Ubuntu Apache packaging is derived. If you can read this page, it means that the Apache HTTP server installed at this site is working properly. You should **replace this file** (located at /var/www/html/index.html) before continuing to operate your HTTP server.

If you are a normal user of this web site and don't know what this page is about, this probably means that the site is currently unavailable due to maintenance. If the problem persists, please contact the site's administrator.

Configuration Overview

Ubuntu's Apache2 default configuration is different from the upstream default configuration, and split into several files optimized for interaction with Ubuntu tools. The configuration system is **fully documented in /usr/share/doc/apache2/README.Debian.gz**. Refer to this for the full documentation. Documentation for the web server itself can be found by accessing the **manual** if the apache2-doc package was installed on this server.

The configuration layout for an Apache2 web server installation on Ubuntu systems is as follows:

```
/etc/apache2/
|-- apache2.conf
|       `-- ports.conf
|-- mods-enabled
|       |-- *.load
|       `-- *.conf
|-- conf-enabled
|       `-- *.conf
|-- sites-enabled
|       `-- *.conf
```

* `apache2.conf` is the main configuration file. It puts the pieces together by including all remaining configuration files when starting up the web server.

Web Server Running

Let's change the default page

```
cd /var/www/html
sudo rm index.html
sudo nano index.html
```

Inside index.html

Find the code here https://raw.githubusercontent.com/jamesfebin/cloud_cake/master/ApacheServer/index.html

```html
<html>

<head>

        <title> This is amazing ! </title> </head>

<body>

<br/>

<br/>

<p style="font-family:Tahoma;font-size:1.8em"> Hey congrats, You got the web server running. Let this take you places. </p>

</body>

</html>
```

Hey congrats, You got the web server running. Let this take you places.

Links

http://mally.stanford.edu/~sr/computing/basic-unix.html

https://www.digitalocean.com/community/tutorials/how-to-install-linux-apache-mysql-php-lamp-stack-on-ubuntu

https://www.lassiemarlowe.com/tutorials/microsoft-azure-setup-ubuntu-vm-and-install-lamp/

https://www.taniarascia.com/getting-started-with-aws-setting-up-a-virtual-server/

#CloudIsaPieceofCake

Make a comic strip with the following characters and share it with the hashtag #CloudIsaPieceofCake

Theme: Virtual Machines

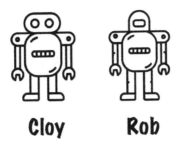

Cloy   Rob

Build a News Reader App – Part 1

In the previous chapter, we started an Apache server and served a basic HTML page. Now let us go way further and build a news reader app.

How shall we start?

We start by sketching the architecture, which gives us clarity on what to build. Start by taking inspiration from a real world example. Understand how they work, then add or remove things based on our requirement.

A newspaper company

Consider how a newspaper company works. They have got multiple sources in different parts of the world, from which they collect news and serves it their customers.

Do we need to build our sources?

Before we build anything, it's better to see if something already exists which we can use, which will lead to easier and faster development. Let us check on the internet if something already exists.

RSS feeds

RSS (Rich Site Summary) is a standard format for delivering updated content. News related sites use this to drive traffic into their sites. It doesn't contain the whole news, but a few things like title, summary, link, images etc.

We will be using the following RSS Feeds

Business

```
http://www.businessstandard.com/rss/home_page_top_stories
```

Tech

```
http://feeds.feedburner.com/TechCrunch/
```

Entertainment

```
http://feeds.feedburner.com/thr/news
```

Sketch Cloud Architecture

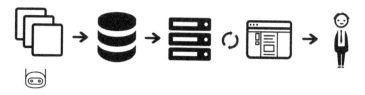

We need to do two things: collect news from multiple sources and serve them to our customers. Technically we require a news aggregator and a web service. A news aggregator can be a python script which runs say every fifteen minutes, collects information from RSS feeds and stores it in the database. Web service is where we serve the news to users. Now we have got good clarity on what needs to be built.

Aggregator

Our aggregator service is required to collect data from multiple sources and update them to our database. First let us look into what data needs to be collected, from that we will make a schema for our database.

Database Schema

Now let us see what data we need, this entirely depends on the functionality of our web app. List down the features of our web app.

Features

1. Show news with title, summary, and image.
2. Should show the latest news and must be ordered with respect to time.
3. The news should be categorized.
4. On click, it should redirect to the specific news article.

The data required are time, summary, image, link, time published and category. We can store all this in a table in our database. Good, let us go ahead and create a database instance on AWS.

Create a database instance on AWS

AWS ▾ | Services ▴ | Edit ▾

Febin John James ▾ N. California ▾ Support ▾

History

RDS
EC2
Console Home

All AWS Services

Compute
Storage & Content Delivery
Database
Networking
Developer Tools
Management Tools
Security & Identity
Analytics
Internet of Things
Mobile Services
Application Services
Enterprise Applications
Game Development

RDS
Amazon Relational Database Service (RDS) makes it easy to set up, operate and scale familiar relational databases in the cloud

DynamoDB
Amazon DynamoDB is a scalable NoSQL data store that manages distributed replicas of your data for high availability.

ElastiCache
Amazon ElastiCache improves application performance by allowing you to retrieve information from an in-memory caching system.

Redshift
Amazon Redshift is a fast, fully managed, petabyte-scale data warehouse that makes it cost-effective to analyze all your data using your existing business intelligence tools

DMS
AWS Database Migration Service (DMS) helps you migrate databases to the cloud easily and securely while minimizing downtime

Services > Database > RDS

Launch Instance

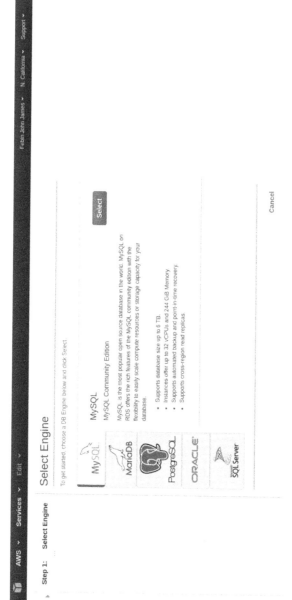

Select MySQL Community Edition

Do you plan to use this database for production purposes?

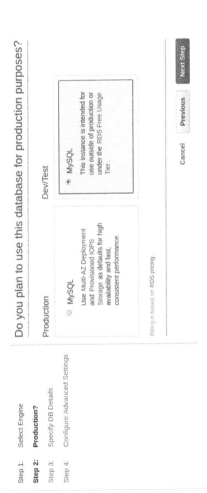

Select Dev/Test > Next Step

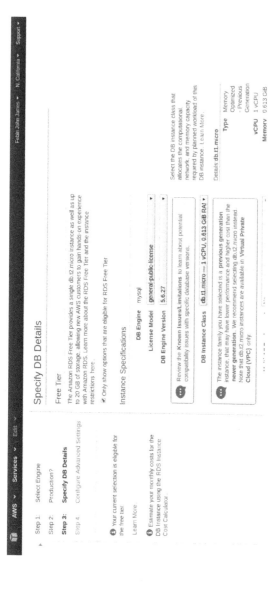

Instance Class: t1.micro

Allocated Storage: 5GB

Database Identifier: myfirstdb

Give a username and password. Make sure you remember this information.

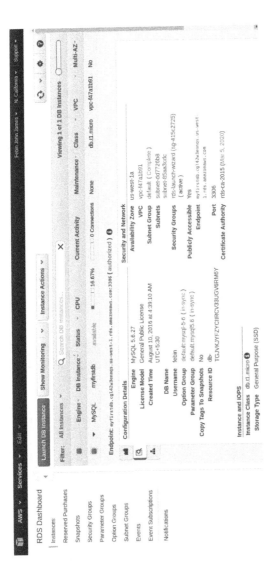

The endpoint is our database's web address. We will be connecting to this address to store and retrieve information.

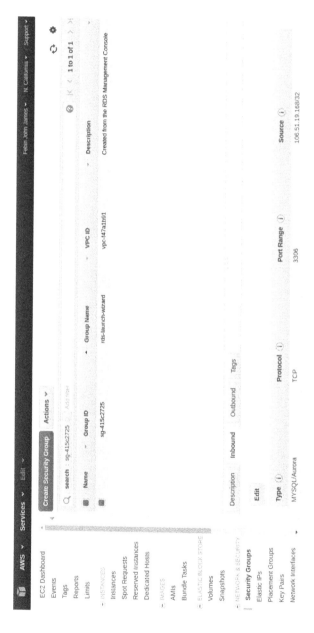

By default for security purposes, AWS blocks all connections to the DB endpoint. We will need to add a security rule to allow connections.

Security Groups > Select rds-launch-wizard > Select inboud tab (bottom) > Edit

Edit inbound rules

Type ⓘ	Protocol ⓘ	Port Range ⓘ	Source ⓘ	
MYSQL/Aurora ▼	TCP	3306	Custom ▼	0.0.0.0/0 ⊗

Add Rule

Cancel Save

Add Rule > 'Protocol TCP and Port 3306` > Save

Install MySQL Client

```
sudo apt-get install mysql-client
```

What is MySQL client?

MySQL client is a program which allows us to connect to our remote database and run queries on it.

Connect to database instance

```
mysql -h YOUR_DB_ENDPOINT -u YOUR_USERNAME -p
```

You will be asked to input your db password.

Create Database

```
CREATE DATABASE myfirstdb;
use myfirstdb;
```

Create News Table

```
CREATE TABLE news (id INT NOT NULL AUTO_INCREMENT,
title TEXT,
summary TEXT,
image TEXT,
link TEXT,
published BIGINT,
category VARCHAR(20),
PRIMARY KEY (id));
```

Install Python

```
sudo add-apt-repository ppa:fkrull/deadsnakes-python2.7
sudo apt-get update
sudo apt-get install python2.7
sudo apt-get -y install python-pip
sudo apt-get -y install libmysqlclient-dev python-dev
```

Install Python Libraries

Create a file called "requirements.txt"

```
nano requirements.txt
```

Now copy, paste the following libraries and save the file

```
MySQL-python==1.2.5
BeautifulSoup==3.2.1
feedparser==5.1.3
httplib2==0.9
python-dateutil==1.5
requests==2.7.0
urllib3==1.9.1
Pillow==2.5.3
```

Run this following command to install all the required libraries

```
sudo pip install -r requirements.txt
```

Aggregator Service

Before we code our aggregator service, let us write a pseudo code. Pseudo code is written in English just for our understanding, which is later converted into real code.

Pseudo Code

Every fifteen minutes

Fetch news from each source

Check if the news already exists in our database

If the news exists ignore it, otherwise perform an insert database query.

Python Code

Find the code here

https://raw.githubusercontent.com/jamesfebin/cloud_
cake/master/Aggregator/aggregator.py

```python
import feedparser
import time
import MySQLdb
import re
from BeautifulSoup import BeautifulSoup
import HTMLParser
import datetime
import urllib, cStringIO
import MySQLdb.cursors
import requests
import json
server='YOUR_DB_SERVER_ADDRESS'
database='YOUR_DATABASE_NAME'
username='YOUR_DB_USER_NAME'
password='YOUR_DB_PASSWORD'
def writeToDatabase(data):
    try :
        client =
MySQLdb.connect(server,username,password,database,
cursorclass=MySQLdb.cursors.DictCursor)
        client.set_character_set('utf8')
        cursor = client.cursor()
        cursor.execute('SET NAMES utf8;')
        cursor.execute('SET CHARACTER SET utf8;')
        cursor.execute('SETcharacter_set_
        connection=utf8;')
        cursor.execute("SELECT * FROM news WHERE
link=%s",(data['link'],))
```

```
        data['published'] = time.time()
        if cursor.rowcount == 0:
            cursor.execute ("INSERT INTO news (title,link,
summary,published, image,category) VALUES
(%s,%s,%s,%s,%s,%s)",(data['title'],data['link'],data
['summary'], data['published'], data['image'], data
['category']))
        client.commit()
    except Exception as e:
        print(e)
def cleanhtml(raw_html):
    cleanr =re.compile('<.*?>')
    cleantext = re.sub(cleanr,'', raw_html)
    return cleantext
sources       =      [{'category':'business','url':'http://
www.business-standard.com/rss/home_page_top_stories.
rss'},{'category':'tech','url':'http://feeds.feedburner.
com/TechCrunch/'}      ,{'category':'entertainment','url':
'http://feeds.feedburner.com/thr/news'}]

for source in sources:
    feedData=feedparser.parse(source['url'])
    for entry in feedData.entries:
        try:
            link = ''
            published = 0
            summary= ''
            title = ''
            image = ''
            if 'link' in entry:
                link = entry.link
            if 'enclosures' in entry:
                enclosures = entry.enclosures
            for enclosure in enclosures:
                    if "image" in enclosure['type'] and
 'href' in enclosure:
                        image = enclosure['href']
                        break
            if 'title' in entry:
```

```
                title = entry.title.
encode('ascii','ignore')
            if 'summary' in entry:
                summary=entry.summary.
encode('ascii','ignore')
            elif 'description' in entry:
                summary=entry.description.
encode('ascii','ignore')
            if summary != '':
                soup = BeautifulSoup(summary)
                urls = soup.findAll("img")
                for urlTag in urls:
                    image = urlTag['src']
                    break
data={'link':link,'summary':summary,'title':title,
'image':image,'category':source['category']}
            writeToDatabase(data)
        except Exception as e:
            print(e)
client.close()
```

Save the file as "aggregator.py" and make sure it is inside home/ubuntu folder

This code runs once, how can I make it run every 15 minutes?

Well, you already know the answer. Don't you? Remember about the cron job scheduler we discussed in the last chapter? We will be asking cron to run our Python script every fifteen minutes.

Open cron

```
sudo crontab -e
```

Write the following script

```
*/15 * * * * /usr/bin/python /home/ubuntu/aggregator.py
```

Save, close and reboot cron service

```
sudo service cron restart
```

Web App

Great, now the only part remaining is our web app where our user visits to read the news. Inside the web app lays the logic to listen to requests from our users, redirect them to respective functions, make connections to the database, fetch results and serve them.

Well, do I have to code all these?

Nope, you don't have to. We have web frameworks and MySQL adapters. They do the weight lifting of listening to requests, redirections and connecting to our database. We only have to write the app logic.

Flask & SQL Alchemy

Flask is a web framework which makes our work a lot easier. It does all the weight lifting of listening to requests on our web server, redirecting them etc. We just have to follow its conventions to write our web app. SQL Alchemy takes the weight lifting of connecting to our database, reconnecting if the connection is lost, etc.

Installing Flask, SQL Alchemy and Other Required Libraries

Create a file called "requirements.txt"

```
nano requirements.txt
```

Now copy, paste the following libraries and save the file

```
click==6.6
Flask==0.11.1
flask-marshmallow==0.7.0
Flask-SQLAlchemy==2.1
```

```
itsdangerous==0.24
Jinja2==2.8
MarkupSafe==0.23
marshmallow==2.9.1
marshmallow-sqlalchemy==0.9.0
MySQL-python==1.2.5
six==1.10.0
SQLAlchemy==1.0.14
Werkzeug==0.11.10
```

Run this following command to install all the required libraries

```
sudo pip install -r requirements.txt
```

Now let us write code for our flask app. You will need to create three files app.py, database.py and models.py all in the same folder.

Python Code

Find the code here

https://raw.githubusercontent.com/jamesfebin/cloud_cake/master/NewsReaderWeb/app.py

```
from flask import Flask,jsonify,render_template,request
from database import init_db
from sqlalchemy.ext.serializer import loads, dumps
from models import News
from flask_marshmallow import Marshmallow
import json
app = Flask(__name__)
ma = Marshmallow(app)
app.config['SQLALCHEMY_POOL_SIZE'] = 100
app.config['SQLALCHEMY_POOL_RECYCLE'] = 280
class NewsSchema(ma.Schema):
    class Meta:
        # Fields to expose
```

```
        fields = ('title', 'summary',
'image','link','category','published')
news_item_schema = NewsSchema()
news_schema = NewsSchema(many=True)
@app.route("/")
def home():
    return 'hey'
@app.route("/api/news")
def news():
    news_type = request.args.get('type')
    if news_type:
        news =  News.query.filter(News.category==news_
type).order_by(News.published.desc()).limit(2).all()
        return news_schema.jsonify(news)
    tech_news = News.query.filter(News.category==
'tech').order_by(News.published.desc()).limit(2).all()
    entertainment_news = News.query.filter(News.
category=='business').order_by(News.published.desc()).
limit(2).all()
    business_news = News.query.filter(News.
category=='entertainment').order_by(News.published.
desc()).limit(2).all()
    news = tech_news + entertainment_news + business_news
    return news_schema.jsonify(news)
if __name__ == "__main__":
    app.run(host='0.0.0.0', port=3000, debug=True)
```

In the first few lines, we import required libraries. `NewsSchema` class is used to give output the data in JSON format.

What is JSON?

JSON is a data interchange format. The format is human readable and hence developer friendly.

Routes

Routes help in defining navigation. In our application, we have two routes. Index route or home route is defined by '/', when the user visits http://yourserverip:3000/, he is taken to the home route which displays a 'Hello'. In the next chapter, we will change this to serve news.

The second route 'api/news' is for the use of machines to read data. Here we are defining an API which will be used in the next chapter to fetch and sync updated data. You can navigate to the API by visiting http://yourserverip:3000/news/api

What is an API?

API (Application Program Interface) is how a program interacts with another program. You might have noticed Facebook login in different websites. Those websites use Facebook's API to validate and fetch information. An API should provide structured data because computers understand only structured information, unlike humans.

Get Request

In 'Get' request we pass parameters along with URL.

```
news_type = request.args.get('type')
if news_type:
        news =
```

```
News.query.filter(News.category==news_type).
order_by(News.published.
desc()).limit(2).all()
```

```
return news_schema.jsonify(news)
```

Here we check if there is a parameter called type, if it exists then show news of that type. The parameter can be passed in the URL. The following URL will only fetch news which belongs to tech category.

```
http://yourserverip:3000/news/api?type=tech
```

Do it yourself

1. Read about 'POST' Request
2. Implement an API using 'POST' method to add news articles manually.

```
database.py
```

Find the code here

```
https://raw.githubusercontent.com/jamesfebin/cloud_cake/
master/NewsReaderWeb/database.py
```

```
from sqlalchemy import create_engine

from sqlalchemy.orm import scoped_session, sessionmaker

from sqlalchemy.ext.declarative import declarative_base

engine = create_engine('mysql://YOUR_DB_USERNAME:YOUR_
DB_PASSWORD@YOUR_DB_ADDRESS:3306/YOUR_DB_NAME',convert_
unicode=True)

db_session = scoped_
session(sessionmaker(autocommit=False,

                                        autoflush=False,

                                        bind=engine))

Base = declarative_base()

Base.query = db_session.query_property()

def init_db():
```

```
    # import all modules here that might define models so
that
    # they will be registered properly on the metadata.
Otherwise
    # you will have to import them first before calling
init_db()
    import models
    Base.metadata.create_all(bind=engine)
```

This above file imports SQL Alchemy libraries and is responsible for connections to the database.

models.py

Find the code here

https://raw.githubusercontent.com/jamesfebin/cloud_cake/master/NewsReaderWeb/models.py

```
from sqlalchemy import Column, Integer, String, Text,
Numeric
from database import Base
from sqlalchemy.inspection import inspect
class News(Base):
    __tablename__ = 'news'
    id = Column(Integer, primary_key=True)
    title = Column(Text)
    summary = Column(Text)
    image = Column(Text)
    link = Column(Text)
    category = Column(String(50))
    published = Column(Numeric)
    def __init__(self, title=None, summary=None,
image=None, link=None, category=None, published=None):
        self.title = title
        self.summary = summary
        self.image = image
```

```
    self.link = link
    self.category = category
    self.published = published
def __repr__(self):
    return '<News %r>' % (self.title)
def to_json(self):
    return dict(id=self.id,
                title=self.title,
                summary=self.summary,
                image=self.image,
                link=self.link,
                category=self.category,
                published=self.published)
```

In the above file we tell SQL Alchemy the structure of our database.

Run flask server

```
sudo python app.py
```

EC2 Instance Security groups

In the previous chapter, we had to add a rule to allow connections to port 80. Likewise, we need to do the same for port 3000. Edit security groups of the EC2 instance.

```
Now visit
http://YOUR_EC2_INSTANCE_IP:3000/api/news
```

← C ⟳ ① 54.183.227.71:3000/api/news   ☆ ≡ 🛱 ⊚ 🛍 ◎ ⋮

```
[
  {
    "category": "tech",
    "image": "https://tctechcrunch2011.files.wordpress.com/2016/08/screen-shot-2016-08-19-at-2-07-39-pm.png?w=666",
    "link": "http://feedproxy.google.com/-r/Techcrunch/-3/dJbnv8zrqcQ/",
    "published": "1471630562.34113",
    "summary": "  Yeah, you could pick up TekServe&#8217;s 35-piece Mac museum (now $29k), but can you really call yourself an
Apple fan if you don&#8217;t own an Apple-1? That earliest of Apple paraphernalia is about as rare as they come, but if act fast
(and drop a boatload of money), you can snap one up now. Fundraising site CharityBuz has one of the super, special, extra limited
edition early computers up&hellip; Read More\n      \n",
    "title": "Theres an Apple-1 up for auction"
  },
  {
    "category": "tech",
    "image": "https://tctechcrunch2011.files.wordpress.com/2016/08/pokesand.gif?w=680",
    "link": "http://feedproxy.google.com/-r/Techcrunch/-3/5M86WMvWhv0/",
    "published": "1471628103.13042",
    "summary": "  The Pokmon Company, what is going on right now. How is it possible that one of the new pocketable monsters you
created for Pokmon Sun/Moon is actually a pile of sand?? Look: What are you doing to me? Do you think this is okay? Here&#8217;s
what the sand blob evolves into when hit with a water attack: THAT&#8217;S A DAMN SANDCASTLE, POKMON! Get it together. Meanwhile,
there are other&hellip; Read More\n      \n",
    "title": "More new Pokmon revealed for Sun and Moon, and one is a pile of sand"
  },
  {
    "category": "business",
    "image": "",
    "link": "http://www.business-standard.com/article/current-affairs/the-spirit-of-sindhu-116081901458_1.html",
    "published": "1471631161.71266",
    "summary": "She fought valiantly and lost yet PV Sindhu creates history for India at the Olympics",
    "title": "The spirit of Sindhu"
  },
  {
    "category": "business",
    "image": "",
    "link": "http://www.business-standard.com/article/companies/realty-sector-likely-to-generate-75-million-jobs-by-2022-kpmg-
116081900778_1.html",
```

Links

http://flask.pocoo.org/docs/0.11/tutorial/

http://code.tutsplus.com/tutorials/creating-a-web-app-from-scratch-using-python-flask-and-mysql--cms-22972

#CloudIsaPieceofCake

Make a comic strip with the following characters and share it with the hashtag #CloudIsaPieceofCake

Theme: API

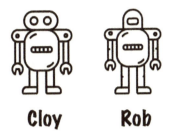

Cloy   Rob

Build a News Reader App – Part 2

In the last chapter, we build an API which gives the latest news. Well, API's are good for computers and developers. It doesn't make sense to users. They need pictures and formatted text. In this chapter, we will build a user interface for our user.

User Interface

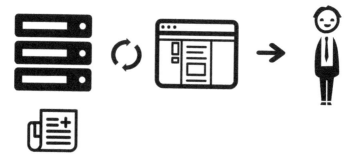

When a user visits our website, we give him the latest news in headlines and pictures. Not only that, if more news arrives this must update in the view.

Isn't that easy?

Consider you send an email to your friend. After you send it, you won't be able to make any changes to the email. If you need to notify the changes, you will have to send another email. Our HTTP server works in a similar way; we need AJAX to update the view without refreshing the web page.

What is AJAX?

AJAX (Asynchronous Javascript and XML) this script will help us communicate to our server in the background and fetch updated data. Once we get the data, we will use jQuery to update the view.

What is jQuery?

jQuery is a JavaScript library which helps us manipulate HTML or the view.

Static Files

Static files are the HTML, js files which get downloaded to the user's computer when they visit our web app. We are sending a HTML file along with JavaScript. The HTML file contains information on how the view must be displayed. The Javascript is used to get news data from the server and update it to the view. We will need to follow flask's convention to serve static files.

Make a directory called 'static'. Inside static folder create a directory called 'js'. Download jquery library, place it inside the 'js' folder and rename it as 'jquery.js'

Make a directory called 'templates'. Place the following file there and name it as 'index.html'

Find the code here

https://raw.githubusercontent.com/jamesfebin/cloud_cake/master/NewsReaderWeb/templates/index.html

```
<script type=text/javascript src="{{
  url_for('static', filename='js/jquery.js') }}"></
script>
  <script type=text/javascript>
```

```
  function capitalize(string)
{
            return string.charAt(0).toUpperCase() +
string.slice(1);
  }
  function fetchAndUpdate()
  {
                $.get( "api/news", function( data ) {

                    var category="";
                    $("#container").empty();
                    for(i=0;i<data.length;i++)
                    {
                            var news_html = "";
                            if(category!=data[i].
category)

                            news_html = "<h1
style='font-size:5em'> "+capitalize(data[i].category) +"
</h1> <br/>";


                            if(data[i].image!="")
                            news_html = news_html +
"<img width=70% src='"+data[i].image+"'/>" ;

                            news_html =  news_html +
"<a style='text-decoration:none;font-size:1.3em' href='"+
data[i].link+ "'>"+ "<p style='color:blue' >" + data[i].
title + "</p></a> <br/> <br/> <br/>"
                                    $("#container").
append(news_html);

                                    category = data[i].
category;

                        }
                });
  }
  $(function() {
        fetchAndUpdate();
        var interval = setInterval(function () {
fetchAndUpdate(); }, 60000);
  });
```

```
  </script>
<body style="font-family:Lato">
 <br/>
   <br/>
<center>
 <div id="container" >
 <br/>
   <br/>
 <br/>
  Loading , please wait ....
 </div>
 </center>
</body>
```

Update the route

Our home route now displays the message 'hey'. This needs to be changed to render the HTML file. Modify the following lines of code in app.py

```
@app.route("/")
def home():
        return render_template('index.html')
```

Fetch every minute

Have a look at the following lines of code

```
$(function() {
        fetchAndUpdate();
        var interval = setInterval(function () {
fetchAndUpdate(); }, 60000);
});
```

After the web page is loaded, we are asking the browser to call 'fetchAndUpdate' function. This updates the latest news to the view. Now, the aggregator we wrote can bring news to our server any minute. To keep the view updated we will call the "fetchAndUpdate" function every minute.

Hmm, but my data won't be very real-time?

Yes, for a news reader app this delay is fine. However you can't use this when real-time data is critical. A messenger app is an example for that. In this case, you will need to use web sockets.

What happens to the news already in the view?

They get replaced. Yes, it is a bad experience. A good way to do is append the news instead of replacing them.

Do it yourself

1. Find out about backbone.js
2. Integrate backbone.js and provide a better user experience.

Upstart

Now, if you close the terminal, the web server stops immediately. To prevent that, we should run it as a service. Upstart helps us in starting our server as in when the system boots up. You just need to configure an upstart script.

Upstart Script

Create an upstart script by making a file called "newsapp. conf" inside "/etc/init" folder.

```
sudo nano /etc/init/newsapp.conf
```

Paste the following contents into the file. Please change the directory structure in the following code to match yours.

```
start on filesystem or runlevel [2345]

stop on shutdown

script

        /usr/bin/python /home/ubuntu/NewsReaderApp/
NewsReaderWeb/app.py

end script
```

Run the service

```
sudo service newsapp restart
```

Now visit

```
http://YOUR_EC2_INSTANCE_IP:3000
```

Tech

How can connect my mobile app to the cloud service?

The API's you build in the last chapter can be used to communicate with the cloud service. You will need to send HTTP requests from your mobile app and you get the response in JSON format.

Authentication

Different users have different news interests. Some prefer tech, some entertainment. A good service will need to understand user's preferences and serve them accordingly. This will require you to store their preferences. Only respective user should be allowed to change their respective preferences. This can be achieved with user accounts.

Do It Yourself

1. Do research on authentication using username and password.

2. Choose a good password hashing mechanism.

3. Modify database to store user info.

4. Implement authentication with the help of flask-login documentation.

5. Give the ability to users to choose their news preferences.

6. Now serve news only after checking user's preference.

Links

```
http://www.w3schools.com/jquery/
```

```
http://backbonejs.org/
```

```
https://www.joezimjs.com/javascript/introduction-to-
backbone-js-part-5-ajax-video-tutorial/
```

```
https://flask-login.readthedocs.io/en/latest/
```

```
http://www.cyberciti.biz/python-tutorials/securely-hash-
passwords-in-python/
```

#CloudIsaPieceofCake

Make a comic strip with the following characters and share it with the hashtag #CloudIsaPieceofCake

Theme: Routes

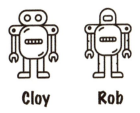

Cloy   Rob

Scale It Up

Load Balancer

Ann is hosting an audition to seek lead actors for her new movie 'Jacob and Angel'. She receives 10,000 applications. She has a team of 100 people to conduct the interviews. An interview lasts for fifteen minutes. Hence only 400 applicants can be interviewed in an hour. She hires a team to make sure the candidates are distributed uniformly across interviewers, and only limited applicants are allowed to enter the interview hall at a given time.

In our scenario, applicants are user requests; interviewers are our servers and the team which manage uniform distribution is the load balancer. Load balancer hence helps to increase the capacity of concurrent users to our web service.

NGINX

NGINX is a popular web server and loadbalancer. It's easily configurable.

```
http {
upstream newsapp {
server server1.yourdomain.com;
server server2.yourdomain.com;
server server3.yourdomain.com;
}
```

```
server {
listen 80;
location / {
proxy_pass http://newsapp;
}
}
}
```

The above code is an Nginx configuration file. Here we are listening to requests on port 80 and distributing the traffic across three servers.

Can we add Nginx to our app?

We can't directly add Nginx to our flask app. Since it serves only static files and doesn't execute python script. However, in order to achieve this we need to install UWSGI server and make it talk to Nginx.

Do it yourself

1. Install uwsgi
2. Configure our flask app to use uwsgi
3. Configure Nginx with uwsgi

Vertical Scaling

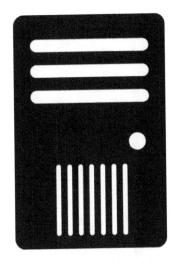

In vertical scaling, we increase the capacity of the existing hardware. Presently we are using t2.micro which has 2GB RAM and 1 CPU. We can request AWS to change our EC2 Instance to say m4.large which has 8GB RAM and 2 CPUs.

Instances Dashboard > Actions > Instance State > Stop

Instances Dashboard > Actions > Instance Settings > Change Instance Type

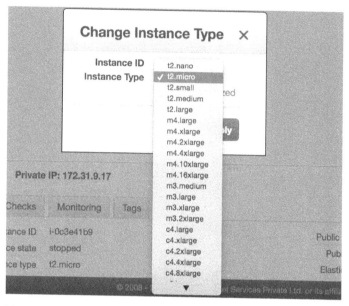

Now you can select instance type of your choice. Remember if you switch out of t2.micro you will be billed.

Horizontal Scaling

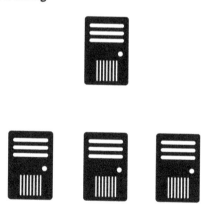

Horizontal scaling is done by adding more instances and using a load balancer to distribute the load uniformly across the instances, which was discussed earlier in this chapter. You will need to add or remove instances based on the load you get. This can be automated. In AWS you can set rules, say if the CPU usage is more than 80% then add one more instance, if it reduces to 20% then remove an instance and so on. This is called auto scaling.

Links

https://www.digitalocean.com/community/tutorials/how-to-serve-flask-applications-with-uwsgi-and-nginx-on-ubuntu-14-04

https://www.youtube.com/watch?v=5swEizOi-kE

#CloudIsaPieceofCake

Make a comic strip with the following characters and share it with the hashtag #CloudIsaPieceofCake

Theme: Load Balancer

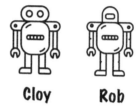

Cloy   **Rob**

Secure Your App

Security Aware Coding

Most of the hackers can hack into cloud apps because coders are not security-aware. Look at the following code.

```
@app.route("/customer/info")
def customer_info():
        customer_id = requests.args.get('customer_id')
        customer_info = Customers.query.filter(Customer.
        id== customer_id).one()
        customer_schema.jsonify(customer)
```

So for a customer of id 5453 will have request URL like this

```
http://server_ip/customer/info?customer_id=5453
```

Now look at the URL, the id is a number. If a hacker notices this, he will immediately try changing the number from 5453 to 5454

```
http://server_ip/customer/info?customer_id=5454
```

This will allow him to fetch details of the customer with id 5454, which he is not supposed to see. Now he can write a script which loops through customer ids and fetches information; he has hacked into a company's confidential data.

This can be preventing by either adding authentication to check if the user has privileges to access the data. A unique string identifier is better than an integer identifier.

SQL Injection

SQL injection is technique through which a hacker views, alters or removes critical data. Hackers use user input to do this. Have a look at the following URL.

```
http://server_ip/customer/info?customer_id=5454;Drop
Table customers
```

Here hacker is passing an SQL command along with customer_id input. If there is no sanitization in input, customers table can get deleted.

Encrypting Credentials

If you check the code in 'app.py' we notice that the MySQL credentials are written in plain text. This is hazardous. A good way to store this information is by encrypting MySQL credentials, and the program should decrypt it at run time. Encryption should also happen when the client and server communicates.

What is encryption?

In the above image when the sentence 'Hey, How are you' is sent, it's possible for hackers to hack into the network and look into the data. To avoid this, we encrypt 'Hey, How are you' with a key say 'mykey1' and the encrypted text will look like '$f834#uejssi288XMn'. Once the recipient receives the information, it uses 'mykey1' to convert '$f834#uejssi288XM' to 'Hey, How are you'. If a hacker peeps into the data, he will see '$f834#uejssi288XMn'. He can't make sense of it.

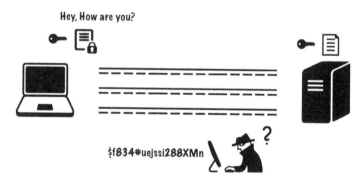

SSL/TLS Encryption

SSL is a protocol for sending confidential information via the internet. SSL certificate helps you encrypt data. You can use letsencrypt to generate SSL certificate, or you can buy one.

Do it yourself

1. Generate an SSL certificate using letsencrypt.
2. Install the certificate on your NGINX server.

Rate Limiting

Rate limiting prevents abuse of server resources. A hacker can flood the resources of a server by generating fake requests; this can be countered by limiting requests for IP addresses. NGINX server can be configured to do this.

Do it yourself

1. Google 'NGINX Rate Limiting'
2. Configure NGINX server for limiting requests to news API

Links

https://certbot.eff.org/

https://lincolnloop.com/blog/rate-limiting-nginx/

#CloudIsaPieceofCake

Make a comic strip with the following characters and share it with the hashtag #CloudIsaPieceofCake

Theme: Encryption

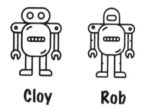

Cloy　　**Rob**

Well, it's an end to the book, but this is a new beginning for you. Use the things you learned to build epic stuff. I would love to see the things you create.

Tell your friends if you like this book, if not tell me. I look forward for your reviews and feedback.

Please feel free to reach me on

Email

jamesfebin@gmail.com

Facebook

facebook.com/heyfebin

Twitter

twitter.com/heyfebin

Blog

febin.work